A Thief Saves the World

Save the World
& Battle Royale Adventures

Book 1

Jamie Sandford

Contents

For Hudson

PART 1 - STONEWOOD

CHAPTER 1

CAUGHT IN THE ACT

As I reached for the prize, I heard the door open and almost immediately the lights came on.

"Stay right where you are Flynn!" came the unmistakable drawl of Mrs. Haggard the orphanage director.

I froze.

Well this was embarrassing. I had been caught with my fingers in the cookie jar...and I'm talking actually in the cookie jar. It was Mrs. Haggard's cookie jar which she kept on her topmost shelf...in her locked office...and it was 1.30 in the morning. Oops.

This was unfortunate, but I didn't panic. I had my back to her, and Mrs. Haggard hadn't seen my face. In a black hoodie and sweatpants she couldn't know for sure it was me (even though it obviously was!), so I still had a slim chance of getting myself out of this.

And that was all I needed.

In one smooth movement I transferred the five cookies from my hand to the pocket of my hoodie and tossed the glass cookie jar lid over my shoulder. I heard Mrs. Haggard gasp and imagined her arms flailing hopelessly, as she attempted to catch the lid. Then came the satisfyingly loud crash, as the lid smashed to the floor and shattered into a thousand pieces.

While Mrs. Haggard howled, I was already on the move, flinging myself back and diving through the same open window I had used to enter the office only minutes earlier. A particularly reckless move, as the director's office was on the 5th floor of the orphanage! I was almost certainly going to end up deader than dead on the pavement below if I didn't get my timing just right.

My right hand grabbed and held the drainpipe that ran down the length of the building, but my left hand slapped against the pipe and slid straight off. My momentum carried the rest of my body and slammed it, full force, into the wall, knocking the breath right out of me. Despite my inability to breathe, the adrenaline coursing through my body helped me to grab again and hold onto the drainpipe.

I'd like to say that I shimmied down the pipe

with grace and style, but frankly it was more of a controlled, bumpy collapse and I was grateful to catch a foothold on the third-floor window ledge. I tumbled through the open window, dropped into the corridor and then on to the floor, my lungs finally filling again as I drew in a large, shuddering breath.

"Everything okay?" asked Timmy.

Timmy was my partner in crime and best pal who cleaned up after me. He always had my back; every criminal mastermind needs a friend like that.

Timmy stepped behind me and closed the window. I didn't have time to stop and chat, I could already hear the thundering footsteps of Mrs. Haggard two flights up. Frankly, I still didn't have enough breath to say anything much, so I gave Tim a brave smile and a thumbs up, while throwing him the cookies for safe keeping.

Picking myself up off the floor I headed for the staircase; now I was in more familiar territory. Swinging myself up onto the bannister I let gravity whisk me down the highly polished wooden rail as it curved down and around the communal staircase, all the way to the ground floor.

I heard a shout from somewhere above me but knew better than to look up and give away my identity. There was just one thing standing between me and safety, and that was Fangs.

Fangs was Mrs. Haggard's dog. After dark he roamed the corridors of the Stonewood Orphanage looking for victims who had made the fatal error of stepping outside of their dormitories. Fangs didn't really mind whether you were out of your room on official business (like going to the toilet) or up to no good. He was only really interested in how fast you could run!

His name wasn't even Fangs, it was Woodsy. We just called him Fangs because that was just about all you could see when he decided to start running after you.

As I dismounted from the bannister and looked along the ground floor corridor, I could see light pouring from two open doorways. Beyond them, the door to the basement, my destination, was shut. Nobody in the orphanage liked going into the dark, dank and dirty basement, which made it the perfect hideout.

If you've ever tried tiptoeing quickly and quietly down a corridor, you'll know how difficult it is and how ridiculous you look. But with the thud, thud, thud of Mrs. Haggard coming down the stairs and a possible homicidal dog waiting to pounce from either of the open doorways, looking silly was the least of my problems.

As I came to the first doorway, I held my breath and peered cautiously into the room. This was the orphanage sick bay and it was mercifully empty.

I moved on to the next doorway which led to the staff kitchen and craned my neck so that I could look into the room while showing as little of myself as possible. And there he was... the hound from hell! Fangs had his face buried in a bowl of dog food and was making a monstrous slurping sound as he hoovered the food into his face.

There was nothing to be done about it, time was not on my side. I had to make it to the basement door pronto before Mrs. Haggard came crashing down the last flight of stairs and apprehended me. Like some deranged ballerina I sprang across the doorway in one untidy leap and, still on tiptoe, padded the final few steps to the door.

Behind me the sound of eating stopped.

The noise of Mrs. Haggard coming down the final

flight of stairs was now reaching a crescendo and the commotion had obviously caught the attention of Fangs. I could hear his claws clip, clip, clipping closer as he trotted to the open doorway to see what was going on.

I reached for the basement door handle and turned it with all the trepidation of a bomb disposal expert about to cut the red wire. The door handle turned, there was a tiny click and the door swung open soundlessly. With all the ninja skills I could muster, I tried to be as one with the door, wrapping my body around and behind it; just a shadow in the night, I hoped.

A bead of sweat trickled down my forehead as I slowly pulled the door closed toward me. Fangs sniffed the air, his ears pricking to attention as he turned his head away from the approaching Mrs. Haggard and directed his gaze toward me and the closing basement door.

Time seemed to slow. Behind Fangs I saw the figure of Mrs. Haggard explode into the corridor from the stairwell. Fangs' laser stare didn't budge from the basement door. His eyes seemed to bore into my soul, even though I was pretty sure he couldn't see me in the darkness.

I backed slowly away from the door and inched myself toward the stairs leading down to the basement. Fangs was now looking at the slightly open door with a quizzical look on his face... and then he started to move slowly toward me.

If he started to run, I was dog meat, so I decided to take evasive action and flee as fast as I could! I flung myself down the pitch-black stairs with predictable results. I don't know how many steps I bounced off on the way down, but when I came to a stop I could feel the cool stone floor of the basement against my face.

No time to adjust my eyes to the darkness, I crawled forward on hands and knees in what I hoped was the direction of the enormous old metal furnace that I knew to be at the back of the basement on the far wall. Was that panting I could hear from the top of the basement steps?

I stopped crawling when my forehead smashed into a brick wall covered in cobwebs, I had missed the furnace. I shuffled to the right, feeling with my hands, and finally touched the cool metal I was looking for. I could hear the clacking of claws on wooden steps.

Feeling my way to the front of the furnace, I scrabbled around looking for the handle of the furnace door. As my hand came to rest on the handle, I heard a low growling from behind me.

I flung open the door and scrambled into the confined and dusty interior of the furnace, swinging the door shut behind me. Almost immediately Fangs was up against the door barking through the grate. Although safe within my metal hideout the noise of his barking reverberated right through my head.

I curled into a ball and clamped my hands over my ears in an attempt to block out the din.

And then the storm hit... and everything changed forever.

Chapter 2

The Storm

With my hands over my ears it took me a couple of seconds to realize the barking had stopped. When I opened my eyes, I fully expected to see Mrs. Haggard standing over me with a grim look on her face, but... I was alone. Strangely, that wasn't a comfort. Where was Fangs?

I peered through the furnace door grate... nothing.

Slowly I eased open the door and craned my neck to listen for signs of life. From the top of the basement stairs I could faintly hear a kind of electrical crackling. There wasn't much light coming down from the top of the basement stairs, but what little there was now seemed to have a purple tinge to it. The purple glow seemed to flicker in time with the electrical crackle. What was going on?

Fangs started barking. He must have returned back upstairs without me noticing and now he was clearly agitated, growling and barking in equal measure.

He sounded... scared.

Suddenly there was a loud crack of thunder, his barks turned to a whimper and Fangs came flying back down the stairs, directly toward me. I slammed the furnace door shut again and waited for his rabid barking, but instead he continued his whimpering and clawed at the grate frantically, pushing his nose into the slots of the door as if he could somehow push his whole body through the tiny slits.

From behind him, at the top of the stairs, I heard some kind of low moaning. Fangs had seen something up in the orphanage which had rattled him to the core.

Fangs and I had never been friends, mortal foes would have been a better description, but right now I could see that he had no interest in hurting me, he desperately needed a place to hide. I didn't know what had spooked a tough demon dog like Fangs, but if he was terrified then I ought to be too. This wasn't a good time to be alone. With trepidation I eased the door open and, without a moment's hesitation, Fangs leapt into the furnace box with me and burrowed his head into my hoodie. I tentatively wrapped my arms round his shivering body and tried to comfort him while he continued to whimper.

"Easy boy, woah, slow down, it's okay. Take it easy." I said.

With both of us now inside the furnace it was a tight squeeze and I could feel Fangs' heart racing as he pressed himself closer.

"Holy cow Fangs, what is it?"

As if trying to answer my question Fangs turned his head and looked back toward the stairs, licking his snout nervously. We stared out through the grate as the moaning noise from above grew louder. And then in the dim light we saw a figure start to descend the stairs. I held my breath. The figure looked a lot like Mrs. Haggard, but only if Mrs. Haggard had lost a lot of weight in the last half an hour! I could make out woman's clothes (was that Mrs. Haggard's hideous floral dress?) but the body underneath was impossibly thin, almost a skeleton. A cold sweat prickled my neck.

The figure lurched down three steps and then froze as if trying to listen for something. I pulled Fangs close to me and froze, trying to make us both as small and as still as possible.

"MmmmWuuurghhh," the figure moaned, deep and loud.

If that was Mrs. Haggard something had gone extremely, horribly wrong.

Fangs started to wiggle and thrash in fear, I wouldn't be able to keep him quiet for much longer.

The hideous apparition turned toward us, seeming to stare directly at us, and then turned and lurched back up the stairs and out of sight.

I relaxed my grip on Fangs who started to whimper softly again. I suddenly felt a wave of exhaustion sweep over me. I didn't know what time it was, but it was certainly way beyond my bedtime. Now that the nervous energy of the last half hour was wearing off, I began to feel more exhausted than I could ever remember feeling in my life. I was also starving. Giving all the cookies to Timmy had been a bad idea.

The crackle of lightning and claps of thunder continued to echo above us. I had never heard a storm like this in the middle of summer.

Venturing out of the basement now was impossible. Who knew what else I would find? Besides, I could barely keep my eyes open. Fangs seemed to have the same idea. Despite the tight space, he managed to turn in a tiny circle and curl up with his head on his paws. I snuggled in behind him and...

CHAPTER 3

A NEW DAWN

... I woke up to dog breath, followed by some slurpy, wet face licking from my new canine friend.

"Yuck! Get off me," I wailed, wiping the slime from my face

Fangs was standing over me with his paws on my shoulders. Directly in my eyeline was the dog tag hanging from his collar. 'Woodsy' it said in gold lettering.

"I suppose you're not going to accept 'Fangs' anymore, heh?"

Woodsy answered by giving me another sloppy lick.

"Okay, okay! Woodsy it is."

Moving was tricky, curled up for so long my legs no longer worked. With all the speed of a sleepy sloth, I unfolded myself into an upright position and emptied myself delicately out of the furnace. Woodsy jumped out and sat next to me, his head cocked as if listening.

It was beyond quiet.

The unnerving purple light was now gone and, in its place, I could now see bright daylight spilling down the stairwell.

But there was no noise whatsoever.

Cautiously, Woodsy and I climbed the stairs and stepped back into the ground floor of the orphanage. It felt like a lifetime ago since I had been in these familiar hallways. And they were no longer familiar, because there was nobody in them. Nothing moved.

"Hello?" I called.

Silence.

At this time of day, or indeed during almost any hour of the day at the Stonewood Orphanage, the hallways would normally be reverberating with the noise of over 100 children and teachers. Without that noise, the building felt very creepy.

We started up the stairs toward my dormitory.

"Timmy?"

As I mentioned, Timmy is my best friend. He and I arrived at the orphanage on the same day, over

5 years ago now, and had been inseparable ever since. We're like Robin Hood and Little John, stealing from the rich (the mean orphanage staff) and giving to the poor (our fellow orphans). If I could find Timmy then, perhaps, I could start to make sense of the craziness.

"Timmy?" I called again.

My voice echoed down the hallways. Nothing.

Up on the second floor all the dormitories were empty. Everyone had probably been evacuated when the storm came. On Timmy's bed, untouched, were the cookies I'd 'found' the night before. I gobbled down three, barely taking a breath. Woodsy took the other two in two quick gulps before jumping up and licking me with thanks.

"Could you find another way to show me you care?"

Woodsy and I searched around the rest of the orphanage, but found no one.

We found some more supplies, including snacks and a couple of bottles of water. I grabbed my backpack from its hook in the hall, threw in the supplies and headed for the front door. I wasn't going to find anymore answers here.

Opening the large double doors of the orphanage I stepped out into the bright sunlight, Woodsy by my side. After a night stuck down in the basement, it felt good to feel the warm sunlight on my face.

Stonewood is a small town, but on a sunny day it should have been bustling with activity. Instead, like the orphanage, everything was eerily silent with no sign of life.

Looking to my left, up toward main street, I could see several cars seemingly abandoned in the middle of the road. And toward the edge of town, despite it being a beautiful summer's day, I could see malevolent, swirling purple clouds, streaked with flashes of lightning.

To my right more abandoned cars and, in the distance, the town hall, the community park and the city clock tower. I wasn't a big fan of the mayor or anyone else down at town hall, but on a day like today I hoped I could find someone down there who would know what was going on; plus, I intended to keep as much distance between me and that purple storm as possible!

I whistled to Woodsy and we set off down the street.

On my way, I passed by the local playground, a favorite hangout for Timmy and me when we were able to sneak out of the orphanage. In the past the playground was always full of moms and their toddlers. Deserted now, the swing set and roundabout looked sad and unloved. The sight spooked me and I scurried on past.

Arriving at the foot of the steps leading up to the town hall I stopped and looked up at the imposing building. I had been down this way a couple of times before. Over the years I had explored most of the city. Timmy liked to stay close to the orphanage and the surrounding neighborhood, but every few weeks I would dare him to explore further afield. Over the months we had roamed all over the city, even venturing as far as the industrial zone and into some of the residential suburbs.

We had been planning an ambitious trip to the outskirts of the city, where I knew there were forests and grasslands to explore, but that plan was definitely on hold for now.

As I looked up at the town hall, I thought I saw something move at one of the windows. I ran up the stairs, I needed to find out what on earth was going on and maybe a grown up to tell me what had happened.

I slowed down as I approached the vast double doors of the town hall and hesitated. What if there was someone inside, but that someone turned out to be another freaky zombie skeleton like the one I'd caught a glimpse of in the orphanage basement.

I paused and looked around. It was good to have Woodsy with me, but if there were monster skeletons around then I was going to need something else to protect myself. Across the street lay a construction site. Like the rest of the city it seemed like all activity had been frozen in time, as if all the workmen had suddenly stopped what they were doing, mid-flow, and gone on a long-extended coffee break. The gate to the construction site was open and within I could see various tools and bits of equipment lying around, as if work was about to resume.

I ran back down the town hall steps and over to the site entrance. I wasn't quite sure what I was looking for, but I figured it ought to be heavy! The first thing I saw was a pickaxe which was perfect, I ran over and swept it up. Or rather I tried to sweep it up, it was a lot heavier than it looked and I could barely raise it above my head. In a fight I didn't think my opponent would be willing to wait five minutes while I attempted to take a swing at them!

A few feet away I spotted some other tools that looked more promising. I picked up a red crowbar with the words 'Mr. Red' printed on it. This was more like it.

"Hello Mr. Red, welcome to the team," I said.

I also found a small socket wrench which I slid easily into my backpack, handle poking out the top for easy access. I wouldn't say I was ready for anything, but if I got into a fight at least I was prepared.

Heading back across the street, I again mounted the steps and pushed at the double doors, which opened with a huge creaking noise.

So much for the element of surprise!

CHAPTER 4

ADULTS, WHAT ARE THEY GOOD FOR?

Once inside, the scene was an increasingly familiar one. Nothing stirred. The last time I had peered into this vast entrance chamber the space had been filled with dozens of men and women going about their business. To see it today, totally empty and silent, was very unsettling.

"Hello?"

My voice echoed back to me from the four corners of the chamber.

Woodsy sniffed his way over to the huge reception desk. Unimpressed he cocked his leg and did a whizz down the side of the expensive wooden panels.

"Couldn't you have done that outside?"

Woodsy looked at me without a flicker of shame.

"Follow me and don't even think of doing a number two!"

I headed for the stairs, the town hall was enormous with dozens of offices and it was going to take a long time to search them all.

On the first floor were some smaller offices, opening each door was enough to show me that every one of them was empty. How did grown-ups force themselves to sit in these tiny rooms every day, it would drive me crazy!

I did come across one room that deserved further investigation, a storeroom! There's something magical about a room full of office supplies, don't you think? The storeroom at the orphanage was always locked. Of course, I'd managed to get in there once, but only long enough to grab a single eraser.

And now, here was an enormous storeroom filled with every conceivable item, everything that you could ever need to run a building as important as the city town hall, all laid out neatly on numerous shelves and in fresh packaging. And it was all mine.

I was going to need a bigger backpack.

Although the temptation was to take everything, I tried, as best I could, to take only what I thought might be useful. I loaded up on batteries, balls of twine and rolls of duct tape. I also found a swish steel-grey colored notebook, with one of those elasticated attachments that kept the book sealed, and a cool, black pen to go with it. Maybe, if I was one of the last boys left in the world, I should start to write a journal!

What about staplers, rulers, glue sticks, paper clips, highlighters, scissors and rubber bands, I hear you cry? Hell yeah, they all found a place in my bag!

My progress through the town hall was a lot slower after that. The weight of my backpack forced the straps to cut into my shoulder blades and walking upstairs was like walking in quicksand.

On the second floor I found larger offices sectioned off into small cubicles with just enough room for one person, a computer screen and a phone. All empty. This was even more depressing then the small offices downstairs! If last night's storm signaled the end of the world perhaps it was no bad thing. At least I'd never have to work in a place like this.

By the time I made it up to the third floor I'd had enough of lugging around my ten-ton backpack. I slung it down and felt an enormous sense of relief, it really was a weight off my shoulders! I should have dropped my pack half an hour ago, it wasn't like there was anyone around to steal it!

As if to prove me wrong, Woodsy started snarling near one of the doors just off to my right.

"What is it, boy?" I asked.

I inched toward the door and pressed my ear to the thick wood. Nothing. And then... a small thud, as if someone had knocked a book to the floor. I gripped Mr. Red tightly. My heart was beating fast as I looked around the landing, checking my escape route in case I had to make a run for it. Holding my breath, I pushed down on the door handle slowly and pushed the door open. Woodsy trotted into the room without a care in the world!

"Woodsy, come back..." I hissed.

Woodsy ignored me and stood in the center of the room, sniffing the air, with his ears pricked up and his eyes scanning the room. I tiptoed in behind him and looked around. This office was huge and much grander than the ones on the floors below. Clearly this was where the important people worked, but the place seemed to be empty.

Just as I was about to head back into the corridor, I heard a faint tippity tappy sound. Woodsy had heard it too, his hearing was a lot better than mine and it was clear that he thought the noise was coming from behind one of the grand desks at the far end of the room. I grabbed him by his collar and, with Mr. Red raised above my head, crept silently over to the side of the desk.

Click, click, click, clickitty, click, click.

I peered slowly behind the desk... and there hunched under the desk, legs pulled up to his chin and hands clasped behind his head was a man in an expensive business suit. His teeth were chattering... actually chattering!

"Yo, dude?"

The man's eyes flicked up to meet mine.

"AHHHHHHHHHHHHHHHHHHH!"

The man screamed as if he'd seen a ghost and, in an attempt to get away, pushed back so hard against the desk that it slid across the carpet a few inches.

"Getawayfromme,   getawayfromme,   getawayfromme!" he shrieked.

"Woah, calm down. I'm not doing anything!"

"This is my hiding place and there's no room for you!"

"Who are you hiding from?"

"The husks, THE HUSKS!" he screamed. "Get out of here before they come back. Leave me alone!"

Jeez, this guy was a mess. Still, one thing was clear, there were more of those creatures around and now they had a name...husks!

"Who are you?" I asked.

"I'm Donald P Beazley, Deputy Mayor of Stonewood and I demand that you get out of my office immediately!"

"Where's the actual Mayor?"

"Gone, they're ALL GONE!"

"Well, doesn't that mean that you're in charge?"

"In charge of what!? A deserted city full of zombies!? And why are you still here? GET OUT!"

Mr. Beazley was shaking and even starting to drool a little bit. Holy Moly, whose bright idea was it to make this man deputy mayor?

"Dude, I'm just a kid and you're a grown-up. Don't you think you should be out there helping kids like me?"

"Forget it kid, it's every man, woman and child for himself. This is my office and there's no room for you or your dog."

"You are seriously lame," I said, heading for the door. "Come on Woodsy, there's no point hanging around here."

"Yeah, that's right, now get going and don't come back!"

Jeez, what a loser!

Heading back to the stairs I heaved my backpack back onto my shoulders. If this was going to be a typical day then the end of the world really did suck.

As I turned to go, the deputy mayor poked his head out from behind his office door.

"Hey you, what have you got in that backpack? You better not have been stealing anything from government premises!"

"Ahhhh, go suck a lemon!"

And with that I headed home.

Chapter 5

If You Build It, They Will Come

Back outside the town hall I sat down on the steps with Woodsy and tucked into my snacks and water. I was feeling pretty down to be honest. I'd lost my best friend Timmy, along with all my other friends at the orphanage, and when I'd finally found somebody, they had turned out to be a complete dork.

I wasn't a big fan of the orphanage director, Mrs. Haggard, but right now I would have given her a big hug if she'd walked around the corner! I really wasn't sure what to do next.

One thing was clear, Woodsy and I were going to need a good supply of food if we were going to last much longer. And, as there weren't any adults to help, we were going to have to take matters into our own hands.

We set off again to find supplies. I didn't want to stray too far from the orphanage so I headed toward the nearby convenience store, not far from the orphanage, where Timmy and I used to buy candy. There was a taco stand next door too, perhaps I could find some food there.

As we approached the convenience store, I saw something that made my blood run cold. Dotted around the entrance to both the store and the taco stand were half a dozen of the zombie monsters, just like the one I had seen briefly in the basement the night before. They were stood so still that, at first, I didn't even register they were there until we were almost on top of them. Woodsy and I froze.

They were ugly, scary fiends. Dressed in the ragged remains of everyday clothes, their skin had a grey-green tinge and they were so emaciated you could see their bones jutting out against their skin. Most horrifying of all were their heads, it was as if their skulls had popped out of their heads and their face and scalps were now hanging from the back of their necks like some Halloween hoodie!

Was this what had happened to everyone? Was the whole world now filled with these creatures? Had poor Timmy been turned into one of these? What were they doing? What was that noise they were making? They seemed to be... snoring?! Yes, that was it, they were fast asleep standing up, swaying ever so gently as they breathed noisily in and out.

These creatures were definitely the 'husks' that Mr. Beazley had been screaming about. He was still a useless chicken, but I could at least understand why he was so scared. The difference between me and Mr. Beazley was that these husks were standing between me and my food and I was going to do something about it!

I retreated back down the street to a little side alley where I found some dumpsters. Rummaging through my backpack I pulled out some of the string that I had found at the town hall earlier. I tied a knot with one end of the string around Woodsy's collar and then wrapped the ball of twine around one of the dumpsters wheels. I didn't want to be without my furry friend, but now was not the time to have a dog anywhere near some sleeping husks. Just one bark and we would all be in trouble.

"Stay boy, look after my backpack."

Woodsy tilted his head and looked at me quizzically.

"It's okay, I'll be back in a minute, just relax."

Woodsy let out a small whimper and laid down; he didn't seem very reassured.

I headed back up the street toward the store. Only a minute ago I'd felt quite confident about sneaking past the husks and grabbing what I needed, I was a pretty good thief after all, but now my courage had deserted me and my legs were starting to feel like jelly.

I edged closer to the husks, in a crouch, moving as quietly as I could. They looked even worse up close! Their snores were super noisy, they reminded me of Fatboy Charlie, one of my friends from the orphanage who I shared a dormitory with. Charlie was a small skinny kid (that's how he got his nickname) but with the loudest snore I'd ever heard. We used to throw our slippers at him to get him to roll over! Charlie, however, was harmless whereas these husks looked pretty deadly.

I headed for a gap between two of the husks and began to tiptoe between them. I was just past them and inching toward the store door when a light breeze whipped up and blew an empty cola tin along the ground toward me. It tinkled and jangled as it bumped along the ground before rolling off the curb with a loud clink.

I held my breath...

One of the husks seemed to rise briefly from his slumber, making a couple of mumbling moans and then... fell back to sleep. I looked around to see if any of the other husks had moved... all clear. I suddenly realized I was still holding my breath. I exhaled and sucked in a breath of fresh air as silently as I could. Without wasting anymore time, I slunk over to the store door, pushed it open and went inside.

Inside the store everything looked exactly as it had just a few days ago when I had last dropped in to buy some bubble gum, but of course it was empty of staff or shoppers. I quickly looked down all the aisles just to make sure there were no husks lurking nearby. Satisfied I was alone, I grabbed a shopping basket and started to load up on food and drink for the coming days.

So, this is what it felt like to be a grown-up. I could choose anything I wanted, there was no one to tell me which cereal I could or couldn't eat. No one to stop me making peanut butter and jelly sandwiches for the rest of my life. I was barely five minutes in and already my basket was almost overflowing with goodies. I paused, maybe ten bags of cheesy puffs was a little unnecessary, maybe I should pick up some actual food. I grabbed some bananas. Right, I was set!

I jogged to the checkout desk to bag my groceries. Hold on, I didn't need bags! I was already stealing the food; I might as well steal the basket as well. Pushing open the door I looked out onto the street, everything was just as it was, the husks were still fast asleep, dreaming of whatever it was that monsters dreamt of (eating children, perhaps?). I crept back past them the same way I'd come earlier.

Wow, this was like taking candy from a baby, this was amazing, I was actually going to be okay! I might only be twelve years old, but I was brave and I was smart and I was going to be just fine. With my shopping basket held in front of me I didn't notice the curb across the street until I had tripped right over it, landing on top of my basket and shooting a bottle of lemonade straight into a wall where it promptly smashed into a million pieces. I didn't need to turn around; I could tell straight away from the loud moans behind me that the husks were no longer asleep. Oh hell!

Without a backward glance I grabbed up the shopping basket and started waddling as fast as I could back to Woodsy. By the time I reached the alley I glanced back and saw that the husks were still some way back. They were coming for me, but at least they didn't move too fast, even with my backpack and the shopping basket I should be able to outrun, or out stagger the husks.

Woodsy was now barking and trying to lick me, pulling hard at the string tied around his collar and the dumpster.

"Calm down Woodsy, not now! We need to get out of here!"

I tried to untie the knot on his collar, but it was pulled too tight now, I couldn't undo it. I grabbed the ball of twine that was wrapped round the dumpster wheel and tried unravelling it. Oh man, the twine was really wrapped up tight to the wheel and I couldn't work out which way to unwind it. Everything I did only seemed to wrap it tighter.

I looked back up the street, the husks were getting closer, they'd be here soon, I had to get away. I shrugged the backpack onto my back and then grabbed the string, pulling it with all my might, trying to snap it off the dumpster.

"Come on, please come on, just snap already!"

I yanked and yanked, but I just ended up hurting my hands while the string remained stubbornly tied to the dumpster and Woodsy. I glanced up, holy cow, the leading husk was only yards away. In that moment, out of ideas, I just froze. This was it; I wasn't even going to survive for one day. Woodsy and I were about to get mangled by the undead!

I pulled the string tight one last time and as I did so I heard a loud swish and, out of the corner of my eye, I saw an enormous machete slash down past my face and easily slice the string. Woodsy, jumped into my arms and nearly knocked me down. I went to reach for the shopping basket but the biggest, most muscular arm I'd ever seen came out of nowhere and snatched it up as if it weighed nothing.

I followed the arm up to its owner and found myself looking up at a man who was well over six-foot-tall, with a body that, perhaps unsurprisingly, was just as big and muscly as his arm. With a rugged face and an impressive handlebar moustache, this was not a man to be messed with.

"Hi?" I squeaked.

"Howdy kiddo, the name's Ramsie and we need to get out of here...NOW."

Chapter 6

Husk-tastic

Before I had a chance to say anything, the human hulk of a man brought the blade of his machete down once again, this time toward my head. I screamed, ducked and then heard a crunch. Whipping around I saw Ramsie's blade embedded in the skull of a husk who had come within inches of grabbing me. The husk shattered and turned to dust.

"Come on!" Ramsie bellowed.

I started to totter forward with Woodsy still in my arms and then felt an almighty shove from behind as Ramsie grabbed the back of my backpack and propelled me forward, half dragging me and half launching me down the side alley.

The rest of the husks were super close now, their hellish chorus of moans rising to a crescendo.

We continued like this, with Ramsie bouncing me along the alley, until we reached the next intersection. Although the husks were fairly slow, we sure weren't moving at full speed either. Had anybody been around to see us, they would have witnessed an extremely odd couple. It's not every day you see a six-foot urban warrior carrying a machete and shopping basket in one hand and a young boy, with a massive backpack and a dog, in the other!

"This way."

Across the street was the Stonewood police station and it was toward this building that we began to bounce. I considered telling Ramsie that if he thought he was going to get any help from the police then he was likely to be disappointed, but I was already having a hard time breathing let alone talking. Besides, I seriously doubted that he was interested in what I had to say.

The entrance to the police station was boarded up with a makeshift wooden wall and an equally makeshift door built into it. Ramsie pulled back a bolt on the door, opened it and ushered me inside.

It was dark inside the station and, after the bright sunlight of the street, I couldn't see anything.

"Watch your step, peanut."

I couldn't even see my feet, how was I supposed to watch my step. I began shuffling to my right until

Ramsie reached out and forcibly dragged me back toward him.

"I said watch your step!"

"Jeez, okay mister."

Woodsy was wriggling, keen to get down, so I held him tighter and placed my hand on Ramsie's back so that I could stick right behind him. Ramsie weaved this way and that until we were well into the main station house lobby. As my eyes became accustomed to the low light, I saw that I was being led behind the big reception desk where the front desk officer would normally sit.

Ramsie dumped me into a big swivel chair, so that I was looking down toward the large front lobby, and then flicked on a light switch behind him. The room's lights flickered on and I could see what we'd walked past. It became very clear why Ramsie had insisted I stick close. Covering the walls, ceiling and floor of the entrance lobby were a selection of blood curdling booby traps that looked like they had been made out of the remains from a scrap yard.

"I made them out of the remains from a scrap yard," Ramsie exclaimed proudly.

"You made all this yourself?" I asked.

"Yup."

"Why?"

Ramsie didn't get a chance to answer because at that moment the husks that had been following us started pounding on the wooden wall at the front of the station. The noise was deafening and alarming. Woodsy started barking and instinctively I started to rise up out of my chair and look for an escape route.

Ramsie kindly but firmly pushed me back down into the chair.

"Just wait," he said.

As the husks attacked the wooden structure pieces of it shattered easily and the wall started to split apart. Within seconds, holes appeared in the wall and the bodies of the ugly apparitions could be seen clearly. Soon the wall collapsed altogether and the husks lumbered through the debris toward us. I gripped Woodsy tightly.

The husks moved forward unopposed and I feared the worst, but then as they entered the main area of the lobby, all hell broke loose. The lead husk stepped onto a slightly raised segment of the floor and was immediately launched, with incredibly force, upwards straight into a bunch of wooden spikes lining the ceiling and promptly disappeared into a cloud of dust. A second, veering to the right, came into contact with a wall and was vaporized by a powerful electrical current. A third stepped onto what looked like an enormous gas stove burner which immediately ignited and frazzled the husk to a crisp. Another husk came to a similar fiery end as it passed under a ceiling contraption that spewed forth flames. Finally, two more husks activated a trip wire, releasing an avalanche of tires from above which flattened them completely.

There was a satisfying silence.

"Wow," I croaked.

"I know, right?"

"How did you do that?"

"20 years in the marine corps... you pick up a few things. Here, lend me a hand getting all this set up again."

For the next hour Ramsie and I cleaned up the mess, reset the traps and built up a new wooden wall to close off the entrance, while Woodsy sat around looking bemused. When we were done, I turned to Ramsie.

"Thanks for all your help, you really saved my behind earlier."

"Think nothing of it, kid, that was fun."

"I'm not sure we think about fun in the same way but thanks anyway. I really need to get home now, any chance you could help me and Woodsy get back to the city orphanage?"

"Sure, I can do that, but why don't we leave it till tomorrow? It'll be dark soon and there's plenty of room here. Stay for the night, I make a pretty mean mac n' cheese and I could use the company."

As if on cue my stomach started rumbling. I'd barely eaten anything substantial in the last 24 hours and keeping my strength up was probably a good idea.

"Sure, that would be great."

Chapter 7

Joe 'Ramsie' Bo

"Choose any room that takes your fancy, except the first one that's mine."

Ramsie jerked his thumb toward a long corridor lined with prison cells. The smell of the place wasn't great, although if I was honest it wasn't a helluva lot worse than the smell of the orphanage dormitories! I flung my backpack and shopping basket down on the bunk of the cell next to Ramsie's and Woodsy made himself comfortable at the end of the bed.

We were in the bowels of the police station and Ramsie had set up a makeshift kitchen in the guard's room. He'd set up a camping gas stove in the middle of the room and was hunched over it cooking up a dinner of mac n' cheese complete with hotdog wieners.

"So, what made you choose here as a base?" I asked innocently.

"Didn't really choose it. I was already here when it all went down - the storm I mean."

"Ah," I said warily, "so, you're a cop?"

Ramsie laughed manically before breaking into a coughing fit.

"Holy moly... no, I was a fully paid up tenant in that very cell right there!" He laughed again. "You wouldn't find a police force in the country willing to hire me, although they could do a lot worse!"

"But I thought you said you were in the marines?"

I started to feel a little uncomfortable, was I about to share dinner with a mass murderer?

"I was kid, but you may come to learn that sometimes folks don't like to deal with what a man becomes after he comes home from war. It's a dirty business and it changes a man. Some folk don't like those changes."

"Why did they lock you up?"

"I couldn't really tell you. They said I was disturbing the peace, but I reckon I was real peaceful when they dragged me off the park bench I was sleeping on."

"You were sleeping rough?"

"I've always been a rough sleeper! Ha, ha. No, I have a home, I built myself a nice camp out in the forest which I like just fine. I was in town picking up some supplies and I thought I'd grab myself a quick nap in the park before I headed home, but apparently that's frowned upon these days. A man can't do anything without causing offense it seems."

I thought about Ramsie minding his own business, trying to catch a few z's in a public park and then I thought about the deputy major, Mr. Beazley, screaming at me for no reason. Sometimes life wasn't fair... not fair at all.

I decided to change the subject.

"So, what now? What are you going to do?"

"I don't rightly know kid. Same as ever I guess, just take each day as it comes. I don't know what's going on any more than you do, so I guess I'll hold tight until things settle down."

Ramsie paused.

"Listen kid, I'm not a great one for giving advice, but if I were you, I'd think seriously about staying put here with me. The world as it is... ain't no place for a young boy to be wandering around on his own."

Ramsie had a point, I'd done a pretty good job of looking after myself within the walls of the orphanage, but things were different now. If I stumbled upon some more of those husks and Ramsie wasn't there... I might not be so lucky a second time. Trouble was I still had something I needed to do.

"That's a very kind offer, Ramsie and I might take you up on it, but first I need to get back to the orphanage. I've lost my friend Timmy and I need to stay around the orphanage in case he shows up."

Ramsie looked down at his feet and didn't say anything.

"What?" I asked

"Nothing," Ramsie replied in almost a whisper.

"You don't think I'm going to find him, do you?"

"Honestly, I don't know, but you've seen for yourself, since the storm came there ain't many people about... and there are lots of husks"

"Well Timmy's smart, if there's a way to stay safe from the storm, like I did, he'll have found it!" I tried to sound more positive than I felt.

"I hope you're right, kid."

"So, you'll help me get back to the orphanage to-morrow?"

"If that's what you want...sure."

"Thanks, Ramsie."

"And you can call me Joe Bo. That's what my buddies from the platoon called me."

"Thanks, Joe Bo."

We finished our meal more or less in silence. Woodsy came and joined us, I had picked up a can of dog food from the convenience store and Woodsy gobbled it down gratefully. He was even more grateful when I let him have one of my wieners. For dessert Joe 'Ramsie' Bo pulled out a couple of Snickers and it was pretty clear from the stupid grin on my face that I was happy.

"The apocalypse ain't so bad is it, kid?"

I had to agree that it had its perks. I helped Joe Bo clean up and then I went and laid down on my bunk to finish the chocolate bar. As I laid there the enormity of the last 24 hours began to sink in.

As a young child I had lost both my parents and now,

in the space of one night, it seemed I had lost nearly everyone else. That was pretty upsetting. Against
that I had found Joe Bo and Woodsy, I was free to
live my life however I wanted. No more being told
what to do by the orphanage staff. They weren't
bad people, I knew that, but I hadn't felt happy for
a long time.

As I finished the last of my chocolate I decided, on
balance, that this was probably what happiness felt
like.

Chapter 8

A Fresh Start

The next morning, I was up bright and early with a spring in my step. The day was full of possibilities and I was keen to see what the world had in store for me; assuming of course that the world didn't plan on dealing me a grisly death at the hands of a horde of husks! After breakfast, we set out into the city.

"If you're gonna make base camp at the orphanage then we need to get you up to speed on building defenses," Ramsie had a big pickaxe in his hands and, as we roamed through the streets, he used it to smash up the town for supplies.

"I'll be showing you how to build walls and simple traps and then it will be up to you to scavenge what you need."

Ramsie started smashing down a tree.

"The first thing you gonna need is plenty of wood. For walls, doors and simple traps, wood is your number one friend. After that, keep your eyes open for nuts and bolts. I see you already picked up batteries and duct tape, that's good, keep doing it."

Ramsie was talking fast and picking up supplies even faster.

"Old mechanical parts are good, don't forget bits of machinery, gizmos and glue. Oh, and bacon, you're gonna need bacon."

"Bacon!?"

"Yeah, I'll explain later. For now, just smash things up, in time you'll learn where to find the resources you need."

My mind was reeling with all this new information. I started to cautiously break up a parking meter with my crowbar. It was hard work and I was soon sweating. Ramsie was sweating too, but it didn't look like he was remotely tired. It looked like this brave new world wasn't going to be so easy after all. We passed the Stonewood clock tower.

"Hey, what about the clock? I bet we could find some useful stuff there," I said.

"Don't touch the clock kiddo. You can hear the bells all round town and that's super useful if you want to be home by sunset."

Ramsie started to break up a car that was stranded in the middle of the road and the car alarm sounded with an ear-splitting shriek.

"You gotta keep your wits about you kid. The noise we're making is loud enough to wake the dead... and I really mean that."

Ramsie wasn't joking, as the car alarm sounded, I saw a husk wander into view and make its way toward us. Ramsie kept on smashing the car and collecting useful supplies.

"Err...Joe Bo?"

It wasn't until the husk was a few feet away that Ramsie took a break from what he was doing and gave his attention to the husk. He swung at the husk as if he was still swinging at the car and within seconds the husk was dust!

We carried on like this for a further hour and, as we made our way from point to point, I started to notice something I had never seen before. Scattered around at random locations were football sized glowing blue orbs. The orbs seemed to pulse with energy.

"Hey, Joe Bo...what's with those blue, glowing things?"

"I don't know kid. They started appearing right after the storm hit. You can pick them up, but I haven't found a use for them yet, so I just leave them alone now."

I spotted one of the orbs a few yards away on top of a car and trotted over to take a closer look. The orb seemed to be giving off a low hum as it undulated and turned slowly in the air, super weird. I reached out to touch it.

"I'm not sure that's such a great idea," Ramsie called out "It seems harmless but there's no way of knowing right now."

I stepped back and continued to stare at the sphere, it had a hypnotic quality to it.

A loud crackling sound off to my left brought me back into the present moment. Looking toward the sound I saw that the purple clouds of the storm had moved much, much closer to us than they had been just minutes earlier. I had only ever seen the storm in the far distance at the edge of town, but now it loomed large in front of me, seeming less than a mile away. How had it moved so fast?

I could see bolts of electrical lightning spitting down from the swirling clouds, they lit up the streets just a couple of blocks away. As the bolts of lightning hit the ground small twirling clouds, like mini tornadoes, appeared and gave off an eerie light. And out of these twisted clouds, husks suddenly began to materialize and stalk up the street toward us!

"Time to go kid. The storm's moving in and we need to get indoors."

I didn't need to be asked twice. I ran back to Ramsie and we jogged away from the storm, back toward the center of town and relative safety.

"That storm's nothing but bad news kid and it can move quickly, make sure you keep an eye on it."

"Is that where the husks are coming from?"

"It sure seems that way to me."

"So maybe that's where all the people went, into the storm I mean, and they're getting sent out of there as husks?"

"I couldn't rightly say, but anything's possible."

I shivered, what a nightmare.

We made it back to the orphanage and I ran inside.

It felt good to be back in my old home.

"Timmy, are you here? Anyone? Is there anyone here?" I yelled.

Woodsy barked as if he too was hoping for a reply... but no answer came back.

I glanced round to look at Ramsie who was staring awkwardly at his feet again. I searched every room of the orphanage to make sure I hadn't missed someone hiding in a closet or under a bed, too scared to make themselves known, but I came up empty. When I got back down to the entrance hall Ramsie had already started setting up some traps and walls to keep out any husks who might wander in off the street. In silence I started to help him. It didn't take us long to rig the place up to Ramsie's satisfaction. He made sure the kitchen was fully stocked and that I knew how to operate the microwave.

I was glum and he could tell.

"I'll ask you one more time, are you sure you wanna stay here on your own?"

"Yeah, I'm sure," I mumbled

"Cheer up kid, I know things look rough right now,

but it's all gonna work out."

"You think so?"

"It always does... one way or another. Well you take care and I'll drop in on you again tomorrow."

"Okay, thanks Joe Bo."

And with that I was back on my own with only Woodsy for company. The day had felt so full of promise, but at that moment the promise seemed to have faded. I had a vision of getting up day after day, just building traps and walls and never seeing another soul, well, another soul other than Ramsie. Ramsie was cool, but a kid needed someone his own age to play with. Where the hell was Timmy?

CHAPTER 9

THE RESISTANCE

That first night back in the orphanage was rough. I tossed and turned in my bed, waking up every time I heard the slightest noise. And every time I woke there was a split second where I forgot what had happened. I'd open my eyes and look over, expecting to see my friends in the other beds around me. Just a split second of normality followed by that sinking feeling... I was alone.

Ramsie did check in on me that day and most days after that. The next couple of weeks unfolded pretty much as I had imagined.

Each morning I would check the traps and barricades to see if they'd been disturbed by husks. Then Woodsy and I would meet up with Ramsie and roam the city looking for supplies. We'd eat together most days and swap stories of our lives before the storm; although I got the feeling that Ramsie was only sharing the stories that were suitable for a twelve-year-old.

Whenever the storm seemed like it was getting close, we'd quit what we were doing and hunker down behind our defenses. A few days into our routine, the storm moved into the center of the city and stayed put for a whole 24 hours. Woodsy and I retreated to the police station with Ramsie and, by the time it was safe to come out, I knew what it felt like to be inside a prison cell with nothing to do but stare at the walls.

Every day I got a little bit better at collecting supplies and a little bit faster at building walls and traps. I also got better at avoiding danger. I kept one eye on the storm at all times and if a husk came into view, I knew exactly how close I could let it get before I had to back off.

I started my diary, but by day 20 I couldn't face writing the same thing over and over… who knew the apocalypse would be so boring! I needn't have worried because on day 23 everything changed again.

I should have known something wasn't right when I opened my eyes and looked at the bedside clock. It said 11 am, I had slept in late, possibly for the first time in my life. I guess there's only so much bad sleep you can get before the body decides to take over!

I'd agreed the day before to meet Ramsie at the police station at 9 am so I was super late. Why hadn't he come by to find me? I pulled my clothes on and headed out the door with Woodsy jogging along besides me. When we reached the police station there was no sign of Ramsie, just a note taped to the door which read...

"Gone looking for some hose, meet me at the fire station."

Heavy duty rubber hosing was as valuable as gold as far as Ramsie was concerned. He used it in his traps, especially traps that used gas, and he was always on the hunt for more. No doubt he was cutting up the fire truck hoses at that very moment. I looked over in the direction of the fire station and that's when my heart sank.

The station was about five blocks away and from where I was standing it looked like the storm had appeared out of nowhere in exactly that location. If Ramsie had been inside the fire station when the storm came in, he could well be stuck there right now.

Ramsie had warned me never to go near the storm, but if he was in it now and on his own I had to try and do something. I picked up Woodsy and stuffed him in my backpack, this was no time for him to be running around.

I ran as fast I could toward the fire station but had to stop when I reached the edge of the storm, about a block away from my destination. The storm seemed especially fierce, lightning crackling everywhere I looked, and on the ground dozens of those mini vortexes were spewing out husks at an alarming rate. I needed to get off the street and up high to get a better view, I considered building a ramp, but I wasn't good enough to get it done fast. Instead I headed for the nearest building and started running up the stairs hoping to make it to the roof.

By the time I'd raced to the top of the fourth floor I was completely winded and had to stop. I leaned against the wall and gasped for breath, Woodsy licked my ear encouragingly.

"Cut it out, Woodsy!"

In front of me was the door to the roof, I leaned forward and tried the door handle.

Locked... typical.

My crowbar was heavy in my hands as I lifted it above my head to smash through the door. I swung once, twice and a third time before the door finally came flying off its hinges.

Immediately a husk that had, presumably, been asleep on the other side of the door, turned and lurched toward me. I screamed and staggered back, almost losing my balance at the top of the stairwell. I grabbed the handrail and managed to steady myself. The husk lunged at me, its mouth wide open, its bony hand reaching for my neck. I tried to pull back, but had nowhere to go without falling back down the stairs.

As the husk's iron grip came down on my neck, I heard a sharp bark and then, out of the corner of my eye, I saw Woodsy jerk forward and clamp his jaws tightly around the husk's wrist. Its bloodshot eyes bulged with shock and pain, forcing it to let go of my neck. I spun around and pushed the husk with all the force I could muster.

The husk flailed its arms and wavered on the spot for a second, trying to regain its balance, before plunging forward, cartwheeling down the stairs and shattering into dust against the far wall. That was too close.

"Good job, Woodsy!"

"Woof!"

Out on the roof the wind from the storm was intense, almost strong enough to blow me off my feet. I braced myself and pushed forward to the edge of the building. This was the first time I had really seen the storm up close and it was terrifying. Above me, the storm had turned the sky purple, its force swirling the clouds into an enormous tornado, lit up with lightning, ready to suck up the entire city. Directly beneath the eye of the storm was the fire station and there on the roof was Ramsie.

Bolts of lightning were striking all around the station, including the roof, and dozens of husks were materializing. I was too far away to see exactly what was going on, but even from this distance I could tell that these husks were not all the same. For a start, amongst the usual skinny husks that I was used to seeing there were now some much bigger, fatter husks. They were slower, but appeared to be much tougher than the others. When they smashed their fists against the walls of the fire station the bricks burst apart faster than Ramsie smashing them with a pickaxe. I saw one appear on the roof a few yards away from Ramsie and it took him three swipes of his machete before the husk crumbled to dust.

Even more alarming was a husk with its head on fire, lobbing fireballs toward Ramsie from a distance. As he couldn't get close to the husk, Ramsie's only defense was to try dodge the fireballs or swipe at them before they hit.

Ramsie was fighting furiously, beating back any husk that came his way, but the sheer number of husks suggested this was not something he could do all day. I felt sick to my stomach. I wouldn't last ten seconds if I ran into the storm, but to just stand here and do nothing was unthinkable.

The rooftop was starting to look a little crowded, there were at least a dozen husks now and they were forcing Ramsie backwards toward the edge of the building. A few more feet and he'd go over the side and plummet to his death. Even if he didn't fall, the fat husks at the base of the building were making quick work of the walls; five more minutes of that and the whole building would collapse.

I was about to throw caution to the wind and race back down to the street when I saw two figures, definitely not husks, appear from behind the fire station. The first was a woman and 'wow' what a woman! Built like a WWE wrestler, she was carrying an enormous Warhammer and swung it around her blond head like it weighed no more than a toothpick. She raced around to the front of the fire station and began to demolish the husks before they could demolish the building. She was so strong that with every swing of her hammer a husk was launched into the air and away across the street.

Her friend was a tall and lean black guy with a massive sword. He was leaping around like a... like a ninja! He had some kind of jet boosters strapped to his calves and every time he jumped, he shot twenty feet into the air. I'd never seen anything like it, this guy was amazing! While his female partner was hammering the husks at the wall, he sprang around smashing to dust the fireball husks that were shooting at Ramsie from a distance. In no time at all the front of the building had been cleared of husks.

At that moment the woman started building ramps upwards to the top of the station. The speed at which she built them was unbelievable, this woman had some incredible construction skills. By the time she had reached halfway up the building, the ninja sprang from the ground to her ramp and then to the roof in two quick bounds. Immediately he started battling alongside Ramsie... they were going to save him.

I turned to leave the roof and it was only then I realized that Ramsie wasn't the only one who needed saving! In the excitement I had forgotten the number one rule... keep your eye on the storm. I hadn't noticed the sky darken above me and now lightning crackled around me and husks started to appear across the roof, blocking my exit back down to the ground.

I was done for! I hadn't been able to save Ramsie and now I couldn't save myself either. I swung my crowbar in front of me hoping to slow down the husks, but they just kept on coming. I wasn't going to go down without a fight, I stepped forward and swung at the head of the husk nearest to me. There was a satisfying pop as the husk's head came away from its shoulders and vanished in a cloud of dust. My swing had thrown me off balance and I fell to the floor, getting to my knees, I swung again and took out the legs of a husk that was bearing down on me. The husks legs disappeared and his torso fell to the ground next to me and disintegrated.

I had done what I could, but now there were four husks grouped together and moving in toward me.

In the few seconds I had left, I pulled the rucksack off my back and pressed Woodsy close to my chest in the vain hope that I could maybe protect him with my body. I knelt over with my eyes shut tight and waited for the end of the world... again!

I heard an incredibly loud cracking sound, followed immediately by several more, and prayed it wasn't the sound of my own bones breaking. And then, nothing but the wind from the storm rushing about my head. I waited, not daring to move.

"Get up soldier!"

Slowly I raised my head and opened my eyes... and there, stood above me, was another woman, the most beautiful woman in the whole world. She was a female soldier with the smile of a goddess. Her dark hair was pulled back in a ponytail, a loose tress fell over her forehead. I was mesmerized by her large brown eyes and the cutest turned up nose above her wide, soft smiling lips. Dressed head to toe in battle fatigues, her toned muscular arms gripped an assault rifle and, and, and... well there were curves everywhere... I blushed red.

"It's okay you're safe now. What's your name?" she said.

"...bleh...aaah...durrr..." I mumbled.

"My name's Commander Ramirez and you need to come with us."

"Huzza...bubba..." My tongue wouldn't work and I went a deeper shade of red.

From behind Commander Ramirez appeared a good-looking guy dressed in a futuristic outfit, complete with gas mask hanging from his neck. He held a pistol up by his head like he was James Bond or something. Probably the Commander's boyfriend... I hated him already.

"Hey kid, stop drooling over the Commander already and tell us your name!"

"My name's Flynn," I said finding my voice, "and who are you calling kid!?" This guy was a piece of work.

The man laughed.

"Okay, tough guy, take it easy. The name's A.C. and like the Commander said it's time to get out of here."

A.C.? Air Conditioner? Abra Cadabra? Ass Clown?

"I'm not going anywhere, I'm here to help my buddy Ramsie," I said pointing over to the Fire Station roof where Ramsie and the ninja guy were finishing off the last of the husks.

"That's really sweet, Flynn," said Commander Ramirez, "but as you see, our friends have already got that covered. Now you really need to come with us, for your own safety."

Ramirez flashed me a killer smile and my stomach did a flip.

"You're very kind Commander, but I really think I'd like to stay with my friend. We've got things set up pretty well here," I said.

"Yeah, it sure didn't look that way when we got here," said A.C. with a smirk. "Enough talking, time to go!"

As he spoke a shiny, steel drone suddenly materialized directly above me and a blinding cone of light spiraled down to envelop me. I turned toward the fire station.

"RAMSIE!" I screamed.

And then everything went white.

PART 2 – HOMEBASE

Chapter 10

The Survivors

For several seconds the only thing left of me was my thoughts. My body had dissolved into a billion atoms, dissolved and sucked up into a white nothingness, all my senses gone, replaced with a vague awareness that I was now part of a high-pitched electrical thrum that vibrated and pulsed.

And I was moving, I didn't understand how I knew that, but I did. Moving at lightning speed, just random pieces of data hurtling along some cosmic fiber optic cable. Maybe I was on the information superhighway to heaven.

It turned out I wasn't.

With a sickening heave the billion atoms that made up my body were suddenly thrown back together in an instant and I found myself back on my knees exactly as I had been just seconds earlier... but now in a completely different place.

As I looked up, trying not to retch, I saw Commander Ramirez and A.C. spring into existence next to me in a haze of shimmering light. Woodsy crawled out of my backpack and shook himself.

"Where are we?" I groaned.

Looking around it appeared we were in some kind of industrial complex, concrete and steel girders lined the walls and ceiling. There was a damp, heaviness to the air, it felt claustrophobic.

Ramirez knelt down and put her hand on my shoulder.

"This is Vindertech Homebase, you'll be safe here, this is where we bring all the survivors," she said kindly.

At the far end of the room a metal door whooshed open with a hiss and a small blue robot floated through the doorway about five feet off the ground, my mouth dropped open.

"Welcome back heroes, that was a job well done, so... well done!" the little robot chirped in a female voice, "and this must be young Flynn? Welcome to Homebase Flynn."

"..." I'd lost the ability to speak again.

Ramirez came to my rescue,

73

"Flynn, this is Ray, she runs things around here. She'll get you set up and I'll check in on you later, okay?"

"I guess," was all I could muster.

A.C. chipped in... "Hey Ray, where's Penny and Ken?"

"They're incoming momentarily."

As if on cue, there was another burst of shimmering light and the two other fighters from the fire station, materialized in front of us. They looked even more impressive up-close.

"Welcome back heroes!" squawked Ray, "Meet our newest survivor and recruit, young Flynn."

"Hey big man, what's up? The name's Ken."

"Oh, aren't you just completely adorable? Get over here and give Aunt Penny a hug!"

Before I could say anything, the formidable Penny stepped forward, scooped me off my feet and pulled me into her ample bosom. For a brief moment I was seriously worried about suffocation, but then Penny pulled me away and planted a big wet kiss on my cheek before plopping me back down on the floor. I felt my cheeks starting to flush again.

"Looks like we got ourselves a player!" said Ken, giving me a wink.

"Okay, okay, give young Flynn some room," said Ray.

I wished she'd cut it out with the 'young', no need to keep going on about it.

"And where is young Flynn's friend? What's his name again?"

"Ramsie," I said, "his friends call him Joe Bo."

"Yes, Ramsie, I though you two were bringing him in?" said Ray turning to Ken and Penny.

Ken shrugged, "We tried Ray, but the dude just ran off as soon as the fighting stopped. We tried to find him, but he vanished back into the city."

This was terrible, I hadn't even wanted to leave Stonewood and now this?

"You've gotta take me back,' I pleaded, "Ramsie's my only friend, we're a team."

"I'm sorry sweetie, but it's far too dangerous for you out there," said Penny, ruffling my hair. I pulled away; I was getting mad now.

"Listen," said Ramirez, "I understand this is all

pretty sudden, but it's really for your own good, and I promise you're going to make a lot of new friends right here."

"Okay, this is all super sweet," said A.C., "but if we're done here, I sure could use something to eat."

"Mmmhmm, I hear you brother," said Ken, "catch you later big man, you take care!"

"Bye bye, sweetheart," said Penny.

They left me alone in the room with Ray and Ramirez.

"Don't worry Commander, I'll take things from here with young Flynn, you go and get some R&R and I'll get our new recruit squared away."

Ramirez, who'd been kneeling next to me, gently brushed my dirty hair back off my forehead. I melted.

"Chin up, kid. I'll check in on you later. For now, just stick with Ray and she'll get you settled in."

And with that, she strode out of the room, the metal door hissing shut behind her.

"So, are you ready Flynn? You're going to love it

here. Wait till you see Homebase, it's wonderful, just wonderful! Your dog is going to love it too."

I suddenly felt very tired. I tried to smile but could only manage a slight grimace. Woodsy barked enthusiastically.

"I'll lead the way," said Ray, "stick close, I don't want to lose you, not after we just found you!"

The metal doors slid open again and Ray floated away. From outside the door I could hear voices, lots of voices. This was the first time I had seen more than one person in weeks. I pulled myself together and followed Ray out through the door, Woodsy keeping pace at my side.

Chapter 11

The Director

Following Ray through the tunnels of Homebase was a shock to my senses. After living a more or less solitary life for the last month I had forgotten what it felt like to be surrounded by other people. The corridors were teaming with folk going about their business and I had to sidestep and dodge just to keep up with Ray. Woodsy barked happily, scampering along beside me. As we whizzed past different rooms, Ray acted as tour guide.

"On the left, you have the cafeteria serving food morning, noon and night. To your right is the laundry area, we'll get you some new clothes from our stores once you're settled in. Over here is the medical center, hopefully you won't need it, and over there is the rec room where you can hang out after work."

"Work?" I asked.

"That's right, young Flynn, we all pull our weight

here, that's the way to run a tight ship. I'm taking you to meet the Director. You can have a chat with him and he'll set you right up."

Work? That didn't sound good. And this Director, he sounded a little too much like Mrs. Haggard from the orphanage. I wasn't at all sure I was going to like it here.

We passed a large workshop with dozens of weapons hanging from cradles on the walls. A skinny girl with red hair, tattoos and dressed in dungarees was busy working away at one of the workshop tables.

"Who's that?" I asked.

"That's Clip, she's our weapons expert and she runs the armory. The armory, young Flynn, is strictly off limits to civilians, heroes only!"

Hmm, interesting.

We carried on with Ray pointing out other places of interest, and everywhere we went there were dozens of people. Some of them I recognized from Stonewood, I even spotted that idiot Mr. Beazley from the town Hall. Maybe Timmy was here. I said a little prayer.

Along with all the normal folk there were also some

distinctly odd-looking people. They had the same clean-cut good looks and impressive physiques as the heroes I had already met, but they were dressed in all manner of strange costumes. I saw two women, one dressed as a bunny rabbit and another as a cute pink teddy bear. A third guy had an enormous marshmallow helmet on his head.

Ray noticed me staring.

"Those young men and women are heroes preparing for Battle Royale training, they'll be heading off to Battle Island pretty soon to compete with other heroes. Who knows young Flynn, perhaps one day you might become a hero?"

Well that certainly made things clearer...not!

Finally, we arrived at a set of doors with the name 'Director' spray painted across them, I guess not everything was hi-tech here. The doors slid open and behind a large, imposing desk sat a man in a waistcoat and tie. With brown skin and a black beard, he had a kind, but serious, face.

"Flynn, this is the Director; Director this is young Flynn. A droid's job is never done, so I'll leave you two to get to know one another," and with that Ray hovered away.

"Take a seat," said the Director in a formal tone of voice. I sat down facing him. Woodsy jumped onto my lap and promptly went to sleep.

"So, Flynn, why don't you tell me a little about yourself."

"Like what?" I asked.

"I'm the general manger here, I take care of Home-base Human Resources and every one of the survivors here is very much a human resource. I like to get to know everyone who arrives so I can decide where they best fit in and whether they need any special training."

I gave the Director a brief summary of my life at the orphanage and my adventures over the previous month. He seemed quite impressed.

"It sounds like you've been busy Flynn, I don't think we're going to have any problem finding something productive for you to do."

"Great!" I said. Maybe I was finally going to get a little respect around here.

"I think we'll start you off working in the kitchens," said the Director.

"Wait...WHAT?" I said.

"Yes indeed, I think a young man with your practical know-how will be a great asset at mealtimes and our dinner ladies could really use another pair of hands."

"But... but... didn't you hear what I said about building traps and scavenging for supplies? I... I'm... I want to be a part of the resistance!" I blurted.

"And you will be, son, everybody who helps out here is part of the resistance, and if you have dreams of being a hero one day... well that's fantastic. I love your ambition, but for now we need you here."

"Aww man, that sucks!"

The Director eyed me silently for a moment, his face suddenly very serious indeed.

"Flynn, about a month ago, the world as we know it came to an end. 98% of the population, as far as we know, vanished and we have no idea where they are or if we're ever going to get them back. There's a storm that grows and moves around, which we can't contain, and it's spewing out husks at a rate that we could never defeat."

"I know all that!" I said.

"So then, you also know that what we're dealing

with here is no joke!" The director leaned forward.

"We need every man, woman and child to do their bit, to do their job. Then maybe we'll have a chance of staying alive and perhaps, one day, defeating this storm."

He sat back in his chair and eyed me. I held his gaze.

"Your job..."

I held my breath.

"...is to help out in the kitchen! Is that clear?"

I slumped in my chair. Woodsy woke up and looked up at me quizzically.

"Yes, sir," I said.

Jeez, this was just like the orphanage...but worse.

"Thank you, Flynn, that's the spirit. Okay, let's show you to your new quarters. I've got a roommate for you that I think you're really going to get on with."

My ears perked up at that. Was it possible that they'd found Timmy and he was waiting for me right now, as we spoke?

I jumped up out of my chair, much to Woodsy's displeasure, and followed the Director out of his office. I thought we were in for another long trudge through Homebase, but after only a minute of walking the Director stopped outside a modest metal door with a door handle. He stepped forward, grabbed the handle and threw open the door. I crossed my fingers.

"Flynn, I'd like you to meet your new roommate and, I hope in the weeks to come, your new best friend!"

And there standing before me, a big cheesy grin on her face, was... a girl.

CHAPTER 12

OLIVIA

"It's a pleasure to make your acquaintance. My name's Olivia Rosemary Matilda Hallewell, but you can just call me Olivia."

Oh, the horror!

"Er... hi," I said staring at my shoes.

"Olivia's been with us now for over three weeks," said the Director, "she was one of the first survivors that we were able to bring back to Homebase. We haven't been able to find her parents yet, but we're going to keep on searching. Olivia's a very brave young girl."

"I just feel very lucky to be here, you've all been super kind," beamed Olivia, 'What about you Flynn?' Are your parents here?"

"I...err..."

The Director stepped in, "Flynn's an orphan, from the Stonewood Orphanage."

"Oh, you poor thing. I'm so sorry."

"Don't worry about it," I said.

"Well for now, I hope you two will consider all of us here at Homebase as your new family. I'll let you guys get to know each other, and later Flynn I'll introduce you to the kitchen staff."

"Thanks," I said, sounding as sarcastic as I dared.

"Oh, and I'm sorry we couldn't give you both separate rooms. We don't usually bunk boys and girls together, but we're running low on space," added the Director.

Olivia giggled, "Oh don't worry, I'm sure Flynn is the perfect gentleman...aren't you Flynn?"

"Sure."

And with that the Director turned and left the room, leaving us alone. There was an awkward silence, I continued to stare at my shoes.

"So..." Olivia began.

"So..." I replied.

The silence was deafening.

"Woof!" barked Woodsy, trying to be helpful, I

guess.

"Oh, your dog's super cute!" cooed Olivia.

She knelt down and Woodsy scooted into her arms, giving her a big, wet lick.

Olivia laughed with delight. "What's he called?"

"Woodsy... he likes you."

"Well, I like him too," Olivia scratched Woodsy behind his ears.

More silence.

"So, you're going to be helping in the kitchen?"

"Yeah, worst luck!"

"You can have my job if you want it?"

"Oh yeah, what is it?"

"I clean the toilets and bathrooms."

"WHAT!?"

"Does that mean you don't want to swap with me?" Olivia said with a smirk.

"No way!"

"That's what I thought," she said. "You don't seem

very happy to be here?"

"I didn't ask to be here. I was doing fine by myself and I want to get back to the orphanage and look for my friend Timmy."

"If your friend is still out there the heroes will find him. You should wait here and see if he turns up. Until then we could be friends, couldn't we?"

"I guess."

"Great!" Olivia said, "I've never had a boy friend before."

"WHOA... who said anything about boyfriend!?"

"Calm down, Romeo! I meant a friend that's a boy."

"Oh... okay."

"Are you hungry? I've got a sandwich if you want it."

In all the excitement I hadn't had a chance to eat anything and now I was ravenous.

"Thank you," I said, trying not to snatch the sandwich out of Olivia's hand.

"You must be tired too. Why don't you relax and I'll see if I can find some food for Woodsy."

Olivia left me on my own and I gulped down the sandwich, barely chewing. She was right, I was exhausted. Once I finished eating, I flopped down on the bed and closed my eyes, I just needed a short nap to get my energy back.

When I next opened my eyes... all the lights were off. I was in darkness.

Chapter 13

Night Ops

Gradually my eyes became accustomed to the darkness. I could make out the shape of Woodsy sleeping, curled up, at the foot of the bed. And across the room I could hear Olivia snoozing softly in her bed. Boy, so much for a short nap. I didn't know what time it was, but it must be late, it felt like the middle of the night.

There was a soft light coming from underneath the door... perfect, it was time for some night ops! I still had my clothes on, although someone had removed my boots, Olivia I guessed. That was fine by me, I needed to be as quiet as possible.

Without waking Woodsy, I hopped off the bed and tiptoed to the door. Opening it silently, I snuck out into the hallway. It must be late because there was no one around. It was time to get out of here, if I could, but first I had a little something I needed to take care of.

I moved down the corridors as quietly as I could, retracing my steps back to the Director's office. I slowed as I reached the Director's door, I needed to get past without activating the sliding doors. From inside I could hear the Director's deep voice, did this guy ever go to sleep?

I squished myself flat against the wall opposite the doors and started to inch myself along the cold, damp surface, eyes fixed on the sliding doors. I was almost past when the doors hissed open. Beyond, I could see the Director sitting in his large office chair with his back to me, talking on the telephone.

By the time he turned around I was gone!

I didn't stop running until I reached my destination... the armory. Ray had made it crystal clear that the armory was out of bounds, so of course that meant I just had to get in there. Besides, before I went back to Stonewood, I was determined to get me one of the super cool assault rifles that Commander Ramirez was toting.

I approached the sliding doors, heart beating fast... nothing happened, the doors were locked. Awww, man. What now? To my right were another set of double doors, I went up to them... nothing. Man, this sucked.

Maybe I hadn't activated the door sensors. I went back to the armory doors and flapped my arms around like an idiot... nada. I was still flapping my arms, like a deranged chicken, when the other set of doors to my right hissed open.

Another flying robot, this one a round red and yellow ball with arms, floated through the doorway and headed toward me. I froze in mid-flap. The bot spotted me, paused, clicked, beeped and whirred a couple of times before moving off down the corridor. I didn't need a second invitation and scuttled through the open doors as they hissed closed again behind me.

I was in a machine workshop, where metal plates, tools, nuts and bolts littered the floor. In the middle of the room an unfinished piece of machinery towered above me and dominated the room. I was out of the corridor, but I still wasn't in the armory. Time to get busy.

Running along the ceiling was a ventilation duct. It ran the length of the room and passed into the wall connecting this workshop with the armory next door. If I could get up and into the duct, I should be able to crawl through to the armory. The machine in the center of the room was directly under the duct, with a bit of luck I might be able to reach the duct from there.

Grates were screwed into the duct at several points, I would need to enter the duct at one of them if I was to get inside. I found an electric screwdriver amongst the tools scattered around the floor and started my ascent up the half-finished machine.

I was almost to the top when the machine started to wobble precariously, I scrambled to the top and leapt for the duct. For a split second I was flying through the air like a bird... then I smashed into the ventilation duct with a thud, sending a cloud of dust into the air. I threw out my hands instinctively, grabbed for the edge of the duct and hung there like a rag doll.

Beneath me the machine tilted violently and, with a terrible creak, tipped over crashing to the floor beneath me... oops. This was not how I'd seen things going.

I hauled myself up onto the top of the duct and crawled carefully along it until I reached one of the grates. I was covered in dirt and dust by this point and sweating like a lunatic. With shaking hands, I leaned over the duct and started to undo the screws that were holding the grate in place. By the time the third screw popped loose, all the blood rushed to my head and I almost fell forwards off the duct. I sat back, my head spinning and took a few deep breaths, this was way more intense than stealing cookies from Mrs. Haggard's office!

Finally, I got the fourth screw out and the grate dropped to the floor with a satisfying clang. Cramming myself into the duct was a struggle and once inside it was pitch black, if this tiny passage didn't lead into the armory, I was going to be seriously annoyed.

On my hands and knees, I inched along the duct trying not to think too hard about the cramped conditions. I passed one grate and then another, I should be close to the wall connecting the machine workshop to the armory. As I crawled on, I heard a tiny scratching behind me.

I stopped and listened; the noise had gone.

I started moving and a few seconds later, there it was again... a faint tapping sound. I stopped, my breathing uneven and ragged. The tapping stopped.

The hairs on my neck started to stand on end. I didn't like that sound at all, something was in here with me and it sounded bigger than a spider! If there was a rat in here, I was going to freak.

I crawled on, at double the pace now, looking, praying for the next grate. The tapping started up again and this time I thought I heard a squeak. Yep, a rat! I had to get out of this duct and now.

Finally, there it was, I saw a dim light from the other side of a grate. Now all I had to do was... oh no, how was I going to undo the screws from the inside!? My heart started racing and, as the scratching got louder, my brain started to short circuit... malfunction, major freak out alert, major freak out alert!

I spun myself round until my feet were aimed toward the grate, braced my back against the duct and kicked out with all the force in my body. It didn't budge. I kicked again and felt the grate bend ever so slightly. I kicked over and over, in a frenzy now, and when it finally gave way, the grate shot across the room and smashed into the far wall. I was so surprised that, for a second, my legs continued to pump against thin air.

Seconds later I was out of the duct and hanging by

my fingers, before dropping to the floor, my heart hammering against my rib cage. I was in.Looking up I saw the beady eyes of a rat staring down at me. Nice try little rodent, but not today.

I was in.

Chapter 14

The Armory

After so much banging and crashing, it was surprising I hadn't woken up the whole of Homebase. I crouched beneath a workshop table for several minutes to calm down and, when I was certain I hadn't raised an alarm, I began to explore.

The workshop was a treasure trove of weaponry. As well as assault rifles, pistols and shot guns there were some serious pieces of hardware. Sniper rifles, grenade and rocket launchers lined the shelves. There were bladed weapons and what looked like futuristic ray guns. I had never even seen a real gun before and here, within reach, was every gun imaginable. My head swam.

"Focus Flynn," I told myself "you can't even lift half these guns!"

I looked around for a light assault rifle, the kind of thing that Ramirez carried. It took me a few minutes to find it, I spent at least one minute staring at a massive handgun with a scope on it, but eventually I found what I was looking for on one of the lower shelves.

Gently, I picked it up. Hmmm, I'd expected it to be heavier, it was hard to believe that this rifle could actually hurt anybody. I raised the rifle up to my shoulder and looked down the sights. I imagined a couple of husks ambling toward me and pretended to take them out.

"Pew...pew-pew-pew... take that, you scrawny husks!"

This was fun, I couldn't wait to see the look on Ramsie's face when I turned up with this. No way was I going to sit around here, cleaning dishes. Stonewood needed a hero and I was it.

"Pew-pew, pew-pew!"

Suddenly, there was a deafening series of cracks and a repeated, hard jab into my right shoulder. I was spun around and almost knocked off my feet. In a panic I gripped the rifle even tighter which set off another long volley of cracks. It was only then that I realized that my finger was pulled down firmly on the trigger.

The rifle had been loaded, with the safety off,

and without noticing my finger had strayed too far toward the trigger, setting off the first series of shots. Now, in my fright, I had pulled down harder on the trigger and couldn't seem to let go. I was spraying bullets all over the place and the force of the gun was spinning me wildly around in circles.

The bullets thudded into the ceiling, ricocheted off cabinets and demolished several shelves, which in turn sent other weapons crashing to the ground. Finally, I lost balance and fell to the ground, the rifle sprang from my grip and clattered harmlessly against a nearby wall.

My ears were ringing and then, as my hearing returned, I registered the wail of a high-pitched alarm. I had definitely woken someone this time!

I scrambled to my feet and scanned the workshop for somewhere to hide. Too late. The metal doors slid open; I was caught red-handed.

Into the workshop strode the Director followed closely by the redheaded girl, Clip, who I'd seen the first time I passed the armory with Ray. The Director had a face like thunder, but I was more worried by Clip, who looked like she was about to explode with rage.

"What on earth have you done!?" she screamed at me.

"I... I..."

"Look at the damage you've done to my workshop. What were you thinking? You could have killed yourself!"

Before I had a chance to answer, the red and yellow ball shaped robot I'd seen earlier, appeared over the Director's shoulder. It was beeping and trilling furiously.

"What!?" said the Director and followed the robot out into the corridor and into the neighboring workshop. This was looking bad. And Clip hadn't finished either.

"There's a reason this armory is off limits. These weapons are for our heroes! How are they supposed to protect us without weapons?"

"Wait, I just wanted to..." I didn't get a chance to finish.

The Director stormed back in and now Ray was with him as well.

"It seems Flynn wasn't satisfied with just wrecking the armory, he's also knocked over the latest storm shield that Pop was working on. That's going to delay his work by at least a week."

"Oh Flynn, this is very disappointing," chirped Ray

"I'm...I'm sorry," I murmured.

"I think we're passed sorry," the Director said grimly, "Ray, go and wake up Ramirez and A.C., get them down here. Pop, go and fetch Olivia, I want to hear what she's got to say about this." The two robots floated away.

"Sir, Olivia had nothing to do with this," I blurted.

"I've heard enough from you for the time being, young man. Take a seat over there in the corner and I'll deal with you shortly," the Director turned his back and spoke to Clip.

Well, it looked like I'd really done it this time. I trudged over to a chair near the corner of the room and slumped down. Man...I hadn't been sent to sit in the corner since grade 5, when Mrs. Haggard had caught me in class with a catapult! I had a bad feeling I was going to get more than just detention.

This was just so unfair, none of this would be happening if they'd just left me alone in Stonewood! Across the room I watched as the Director continued to talk to Clip in a low voice. Clip just stood quietly, looking at me with a solemn look on her face.

CHAPTER 15

THE VERDICT

After a few minutes, during which I felt like a convict waiting for my day in court, the room started to fill with familiar faces. First up was the robot Pop, followed closely by Olivia, who looked sleepy and confused. When she saw me, she gave me a 'what the hell is going on?' look. I just shrugged back in response.

Then came Ramirez and A.C., followed by Ray. A.C. smirked and gave me a wink; was he impressed? Ramirez looked far more serious, if I wanted to impress her this clearly hadn't been the best way. The Director brought the meeting to order.

"Right, you all know this young man. While I'm sympathetic to his age and situation, I cannot overlook the fact that he's been with us for less than twenty-four hours and has already made quite a name for himself for all the wrong reasons."

I held my breath as the Director paused to consider

his verdict.

"I'm tempted to send him back to Stonewood to see how he likes it back out there with the husks, but as that's what he would like, I won't be giving him that satisfaction. Besides, I don't intend to be remembered as the man who let a twelve-year-old get eaten by husks! Therefore, the only reasonable solution I can suggest is that we put Flynn under lock and key, in the brig, until such time as he can persuade me that he's learnt his lesson."

I couldn't believe it; he was going to put me in a jail cell!

"Wait, I want to say something," piped up Olivia.

"Go ahead," said the Director.

"I think this might be my fault. Flynn and I had an argument, he said he wanted to go back to Stonewood to find his friend and I said that if he didn't want to be my friend then he should just go back to where he came from. That was mean of me, I'm sorry I said that." Olivia looked over and smiled sadly at me.

She was lying for me, making herself look bad to try and help me out. No one had ever done that for me before. Now I felt really bad.

"That's not true," I said, "Olivia's been really kind. It was all my idea and I'm really sorry."

There was a silence in the room while the Director considered his response.

"Your honesty is a credit to you. Flynn," he said, "however, we're in the middle of a fight to save humanity and I can't allow any single person to put that in jeopardy. For now, I'm going to put you in solitary confinement until we believe you can be trusted. Ray, take him to the lockup."

At that moment a loud siren started up, much more urgent than the previous alarm, and a red warning light on the ceiling started to pulse on and off.

"What is it Ray?" snapped Commander Ramirez.

"Hold on, I'm receiving the incoming alert now," said Ray, "Oh no, Ken and Penny are in trouble!"

Ramirez ran over to a monitor on one of the walls.

"Get it up on the screen, Ray," she barked.

"Transferring incoming data now."

The screen flickered to life and a grainy image appeared. It was Penny and, as she talked, I could see Ken in the background fighting off several husks.

"Commander, Ken and I are in Stonewood, just a routine mission to fight the storm, but we've run into trouble. We've deployed the ATLAS and built our defenses, but we need some BluGlo. Ken found some in an office block, but before he had a chance to grab it the building came down. Now the whole area is hot with husks and if we can't get to the BluGlo we're going to lose the ATLAS. We can still see the BluGlo, it's at the base of the ruined building, but we can't get to it, there's too much debris in the way. Please advise."

Ramirez didn't hesitate.

"It's too dangerous, you need to get yourselves out of there. We can come back and try again later."

As Ramirez spoke, we could make out Penny turn and smash a husk with her hammer. She turned back to us.

"Negative, Commander. If we lose the ATLAS now it could be a week before we can deploy another one and there are survivors down here. If we leave now, before we've pushed back the storm, they might not make it."

"If we lose you and Ken it'll be even worse. Grab any survivors you can see and get back here, that's an order," Ramirez snapped.

"Wait," said A.C.

He was looking up at the ventilation duct I had crawled through to get into the armory. He looked over to me.

"Is that how you got in here, kid?"

I nodded.

"No way, A.C. Don't even think it," said Ramirez.

"Hey, I'm just offering up a solution, besides if this kid thinks he's such a hero, now he's got a chance to prove it!"

"What are you suggesting?" said the Director.

"The boy might not be much good with a gun, but clearly he makes a decent thief. He seems to be able to break into anywhere. Perhaps he's small enough to sneak into that wreaked building and retrieve the BluGlo."

"You're crazy," said Ramirez, "it's way too dangerous."

"No," I blurted, "I can do it, I want to do it. Please let me try."

"Yes, let him try," said Olivia.

Penny's voice broke through.

"Could you make a decision quickly? Things are getting pretty hectic down here. Please send back up as soon as…"

The picture started to break up and then the screen went black.

"Ray, prepare to transport us down there. A.C. get ready," ordered Ramirez.

"What about the boy?" said A.C.

There was a pause. Ramirez looked at me, calculating the odds.

"Flynn, get some darn shoes on. You're coming with us."

"Yes!" I said, punching the air.

Ramirez had a face like thunder.

"You stay right by my side the whole time and do exactly what I say. One step out of line and I'll have Ray bring you straight back here and into lock-up."

"Yes ma'am."

Chapter 16

Battle Ready

Once Ramirez had made her decision, things moved really fast. Ray and the Director headed to the Homebase control center to oversee operations, while Ramirez and A.C. got themselves battle ready. With Olivia, I raced back to our quarters to prepare.

Woodsy was sat on my bunk wagging his tail and barking with excitement.

"Sorry, Woodsy. I can't take you with me this time. Look after Olivia, hopefully I'll see you later."

As I sat on the bunk Woodsy jumped up and licked my ear.

"Jeez, thanks Woodsy, but that really doesn't help."

I emptied out my backpack and pulled my boots on, wishing I had time for a shower and a fresh change of clothes. Hopefully I didn't smell too much; would Commander Ramirez let me save the world if I was smelly?

I turned to Olivia.

"Thank you for covering for me."

"That's what friends do, right?" she said with a sweet smile.

"I guess. I've not had that many friends."

"Well, just come back in one piece and I'm sure you'll make a whole bunch more."

"Thanks," I said again.

"We better get a move on; they'll be waiting for us."

Olivia led the way as we ran down the corridors. Anxious faces turned to watch us as we scooted by, I wondered what I had gotten myself into. Maybe working in the kitchens wasn't such a bad idea after all. Too late for that now.

When we reached the transportation center Commander Ramirez and A.C. were already there and waiting to go. They were in full battle gear with an array of weapons and equipment strapped to their backs. With expressions of grim determination, they looked ready for business. Now I was nervous, all I had was an empty backpack.

"Get over here next to me," ordered Ramirez, "Ray, are you ready to go?"

Ray's voice came over the intercom systems.

"We're ready Commander, just say the word. I'm dropping you right on top of Ken and Penny, so be ready for incoming as soon as you touch down."

"Copy that," said Ramirez, "okay, stand by A.C., Flynn, remember what I said, stick to me like glue."

"Yes, Commander."

A.C. leaned over, smiling, and whispered in my ear.

"Well, little thief, now we're gonna see what you're made of."

"Hit it, Ray," barked Ramirez.

The dazzling bright light flickered above our heads. I swallowed hard. As the warm light engulfed us, I had time for one last prayer. Please let me get out of this alive.

And then, once again, everything went white.

Chapter 17

Fighting the Storm

Although I knew what was happening, teleportation was no easier the second time around. Once again, I experienced the unnerving sensation of being turned inside out and every atom of my being scattered into the cosmos...totally weird.

Once airborne, so to speak, there was a sense of peace, as my mind floated through space and time, but this peace was rudely interrupted when I was harshly reorganized into my physical self and dumped unceremoniously into the carnage of war.

The noise was intense and deafening, I was back in Stonewood, but my surroundings were unrecognizable. All around me the buildings were in various states of disrepair, rubble and debris everywhere.

Directly behind me was a building that had completely collapsed, this must be the office block that Penny had described earlier. Where there had once been a tall building, with perhaps three or four storeys, there was now a mountain shaped pile of twisted metal, concrete, glass and bricks. If the BluGlo was under that lot I couldn't imagine how I was supposed to get to it.

And that was the least of our problems.

I crouched down on a small pile of debris and to my left and right, behind and in front, stood the heroes, Commander Ramirez, A.C., Penny and Ken. And beyond them was an endless sea of moaning husks, totally encircling us and moving steadily, inexhaustibly toward me.

The heroes were already defending our position. Hammers and swords swung, assault rifles and laser guns blasted away and husks were smashed to dust. The husks appeared to be no match for our heroes, but the tide of the undead was so large it didn't seem possible that my friends could fend them off forever.

"Retreat slowly toward the base of the building," Ramirez shouted over the din, "Flynn, stay within our perimeter."

The five of us moved slowly toward the twisted remains of the office block, while the savage fighting continued all around. A husk, who had edged toward a gap between the fighters, was almost within touching distance before Ken noticed and sliced it in two with his heavy sword.

"Thanks," I said, "that was close."

"No problem, little man, just keep moving," Ken replied.

When we reached the foot of what used to be the building, we slowly climbed up the pile of rubble. At this point the going got hard, the surface was uneven and debris was shifting under our weight. Twice I put my foot down only to have a brick or piece of plaster give way, sending me off balance.

Eventually, we reached a section of the rubble about twelve feet off the ground and I suddenly saw it. Through the tangle of metal and concrete I could make out a faint, pulsing blue glow. Clearly the BluGlo wasn't completely buried within the ruined building, but that still didn't explain how I was supposed to reach it.

"Cover for me," screamed Ramirez.

There was no longer a husk threat from above us, so the other heroes arranged themselves in a triangle in front of Ramirez and continued to fight the threat from below.

Ramirez crawled over the steep slope, stopping occasionally to peer into the darkness and toward the blue light. She stopped at a slab of concrete, about the size of a manhole cover, and pulled at it, prizing it away from the rest of the debris.

"Give me a hand," she grunted as she braced herself and tried to lever the concrete aside.

I got behind the slab and used my legs to push, it didn't want to move.

"On three. One, two, three!"

We both strained as hard as we could and slowly, painfully the concrete shifted. With every last bit of strength I pushed with my legs, while Ramirez pulled, until the heavy piece of rubble dislodged and toppled slowly down the slope. With the slab gone a small passage was revealed, a small hole that vanished into darkness.

"Please tell me that's not the way in?" I wheezed.

"Sorry Flynn, that's the best we can do right now. I can't see if there's room for you to make it all the way to the BluGlo, but all you have to do is try. If you can't get through, just turn right around and come back, don't take any risks. We can't afford for you to get stuck under there as well. Here, take this."

She handed me a small head torch, complete with elastic head band which I pulled down onto my forehead and tightened via a clasp at the back.

"What about you guys?" I asked.

"Don't worry about us, darling," this was Penny, "you just do your best and we'll be waiting for you when you get back. I've got complete faith in you."

"I'm glad someone has," I replied, moving shakily toward the narrow opening.

As I was about to crawl forwards into the gap, Ramirez lowered her head close to mine.

"Take good care and come back safe," she breathed into my ear.

I felt the hairs on the back of my neck stand on end. Despite the commotion, her voice calmed my fear and gave me the courage to dip my arms, and then my head, into the jagged gap in the debris and into darkness.

CHAPTER 18

A THIEF SAVES THE WORLD

Within seconds of entering the hole, my courage turned back to fear and I felt panic rise up in my chest. This was nothing like the ventilation duct I had crawled through back at Homebase, in fact this was nothing like anything I had attempted in my life.

Once inside the remains of the building the noise levels dipped to a distant roar. I could hear my ragged breathing, made all the more difficult by the thick, dry dust swimming in the air around me.

In the distance I saw the BluGlo more clearly now, but my route to it was far less clear. I inched forward on my knees and elbows, banishing any thoughts of claustrophobia. I felt the imposing weight of the concrete above me. If what remained of the building was to move or shift, I would be squashed flat.

The head torch was bright but only lit up a small

area directly in front of me, everything outside its narrow beam was pitch black

After a few meters, my path forward was blocked by a mesh of thick steel wires, the stuff used to reinforce concrete, and for a moment I thought my mission was finished before it had even begun. Then, as I turned my head, I noticed another opening to my right, but this one headed straight down. I poked my head into it and looked in. I couldn't see the bottom, not a good sign.

There was no room to turn myself around and lower myself in feet first, so I inched myself vertically down into the hole, hoping against hope that I could brace myself with my arms and legs as I descended.

I was now upside down and the blood rushed to my head, making my temples thud with the sound of my own heartbeat. My arms shook as they took the strain and drops of sweat ran down off my forehead and into my eyes. I had made a serious misjudgment.

Suddenly my hand slipped and I plunged forward. I pressed my arms and legs against the tunnel walls to stop myself falling further, but gravity had hold of me now and I accelerated quickly. Without warning the tunnel widened and for a split second I was in freefall.

I landed on my back, the impact knocking the breath right out of my body and leaving me gasping for air. I curled into a ball and just lay there getting my bearings. Looking up, I saw that the entrance to the tunnel I had fallen from was just five feet above me. The fall hadn't killed me, that was the good news, but as I moved a wave of nausea rolled up from my stomach, forcing me to lay still again.

I gently turned my head left and right, the head torch illuminating my cramped surroundings. I seemed to be in the remains of a room, laying on a small patch of tiled floor strewn with debris. Over three quarters of the room had been demolished, including the ceiling. When the building had collapsed several iron girders and a mesh of metal reinforcement had fallen in such a way as to preserve this pocket of space that I was now lying in.

Carefully, with a groan of pain, I rolled on to my side. Behind me and to my right was a slope of rubble, formed by the collapsed walls and ceiling. And there, slowly spinning in the air at the top of the slope, was the BluGlo. By luck rather than judgement, I had done it. I was within reach of my prize.

I dragged myself to my knees and felt a sharp pain shoot through my bruised ribs. I tried to stand up, but my right ankle gave way and I slumped to my knees again. It didn't seem broken, I was sure I'd be in a lot more pain if it was, but I had twisted it badly during the fall.

I'd found the BluGlo, but it wasn't clear that I would have the strength to get it out of here. Slowly, agonizingly slowly, I crawled up the slope toward it, the sharp rocks cutting into my arms and legs.

As I reached the top of the slope, now within a foot of the BluGlo, I heard a scraping sound to my left and then saw a small pile of bricks start to move. With renewed urgency I pushed on and as I reached the BluGlo I tentatively reached out for it. It felt warm to the touch and gave off a low hum, like a soft rubber ball of energy. Quickly, I dragged it toward my chest and shrugged off my empty backpack, shoving it inside and fastening it closed.

I threw my backpack down the slope where it came to a stop directly below my escape route. I followed it back down the slope on my backside, keeping as much weight off my throbbing ankle as possible.

As I reached the floor, the bricks halfway up the

slope moved again, and then from beneath a withered hand shot upwards and clawed at the air. A husk buried in the rubble was now pushing up and out of its concrete prison.

CHAPTER 19

THE GREAT ESCAPE

This was just ridiculous! I had risked life and limb to crawl into the remains of a demolished building and here, in my moment of triumph, battered, bruised and buried under several tons of concrete, I was going to end up as dinner for a mindless, groaning husk!

No way was I going to let that happen.

I limped over to my backpack and stuffed it upwards into the tunnel just above my head. Step one complete! Now all I had to do was figure a way to pull myself back up to safety. The tunnel entrance was just a foot too high for me to gain a good, strong handhold, I needed something to stand on.

Behind me the husk had now wiggled halfway out of its rocky lair and would soon be free. Darn husks! I picked up a broken piece of brick and threw it as hard as I could at the husk. It bounced off its head with a satisfying 'thunk', but apart from stunning the husk momentarily it did little to slow its progress.

I searched around frantically for something to stand on, my eyes finally spotting a chair leg sticking out of the debris. I grabbed it and heaved with all my strength, the pain in my ankle now forgotten as panic and dread set in.

The leg, along with the rest of the chair, came flying out of the wreckage way more easily than I had anticipated and I went sprawling, landing in a heap with the chair on top of me.

The husk was now hobbling down the slope toward me. I picked myself up, grabbed the chair and ran at the husk, wailing like a banshee. Hitting the husk full in the chest, I knocked it off its feet and back up the slope where it lay, thrashing its arms and legs.

Quickly I placed the chair under the tunnel entrance, stood on it and shoved my backpack another couple of feet up the narrow passage, before bracing myself against the side of the tunnel and climbing up to join it.

Slowly and painfully, pushing the backpack further upwards with my head, I scrabbled desperately up the tunnel. The husk clawed and moaned beneath me, ready to punish any misstep. My twisted ankle, revolted by the climb, blazed with pain. I felt sick.

My body shook with the exertion. On the verge of collapse, the husk still raging below me, I strained and pushed upwards with one last effort. The backpack popped forward, finally free, and there, just inches above me, was the lip of the tunnel. I threw one hand, then the other, grasping for purchase until, with a heave and a cry of relief, I pulled myself back to relative safety.

Exhausted, I lay panting for several seconds, summoning up the energy to crawl the final few feet back to freedom. I could make out distant voices and the promise of fresh air. Someone was calling my name. I had to get out of here.

Grunting and squirming, I crawled forward pushing my backpack and its precious cargo in front of me. With every foot covered the noise of battle became louder, but I welcomed it now. Anything was better than being stuck in this tomb a moment longer.

And then I saw her face again, Commander Ramirez hunched by the tunnel entrance, looking toward me and calling my name. They were still there, waiting for me, just liked they'd promised. It was going to be alright. I was going to be alright.

And I had done it, I had found the BluGlo and brought it back.

I kept crawling forward, in a daze now, my arms and legs moving automatically without me thinking about it. Then I was out, arms pulling me upward, out into the air and the cacophony of noise and chaos.

When I came to my senses, I found myself hanging off A.C.'s back, my arms wrapped around his neck. He turned his eyes to meet mine.

"Not bad kid, not bad at all," he said with a grin.

Across the way Ken was placing the BluGlo into some contraption, while Penny built defenses around it. Next to me Ramirez was shouting.

"Now Ray, get us out of here now!"

From far away I thought I heard someone calling my name. As the transportation drones appeared above our heads and started to produce their swirling white light, I heard it again.

"Flynn, wait. Over here Flynn. Look over here!"

I turned my head, as the white light started to en-circle us, and looked toward the voice. Behind me the collapsed building rose up before me. I lifted my gaze to the summit and blinked hard, not trus-ting my own eyes. As the storm clouds parted, a ray of sunlight broke through, illuminating the moun-tainous pile. And there, like a colossus bestriding the earth, stood Ramsie, a triumphant smile etched across his face.

In his arms, waving and still shouting my name, was Timmy!

END OF BOOK 1

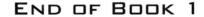

NOTE FROM THE AUTHOR

Thank you so much for buying my book, I hope you enjoyed it.

If you did please leave a positive review. Reviews really help independent authors to find new readers.

Book 2 of the series is on its way. I would love to hear from any fans. Let me know what and who you would like to see in the next book.

You can contact me at jamiesandford@gmail.com

Thanks for reading!

Printed in Great Britain
by Amazon